i matter

i matter
a reminder....

- terri st.cloud

bone sigh books

copyright 2008
all rights reserved
printed in the USA

ISBN: 978-0-9815440-5-2 (pbk)
bone sigh arts
www.bonesigharts.com
www.bonesighbooks.com

cover art: yohan
www.bfg-productions.com

book layout / design:
zakk and yo
www.mazuzu.com

contents

contents

there's someone who needs to know that she matters.
we're still working on it, and i'm trying to help her
get there....it is to her, that i offer this book.

little terri, i treasure you.
this book is yours.

a lot of things happened in my life when i started to figure out that i mattered. explosions, new worlds opening, old worlds closing....sometimes i think that my heart cracked wide open back then.

as i write this, it's been over seven years since the poem 'i matter' was born. i feel like an entirely different person from that woman who sat at my kitchen table so many years ago with tears in her eyes as her heart began to split open.

i don't really understand the growth process and how we become who we are and how parts of us stay and other parts get discarded. i do know it's so much more work than i ever could have imagined to try to become healthy. and i'm thinking that there's a whole lot of us out there who have struggled or are struggling with the idea that we matter.

sometimes it just may take a split open heart to get us to where we need to go....and that tiny little seed of knowing that we're worth more than what is now present.

i haven't gotten it down in my bones like i want to. i still struggle constantly. i've come a long way....but see the very long way left ahead of me. and the more i talk to people about this, the more i see i'm not alone.

the following collection of poems comes from my journey within. i'm not 'there' yet and as i travel, i begin to understand more and more that perhaps there never will be a 'there'... just more and more journeying.

if we travel with the knowledge that we matter, then the paths seem to take a new life of their own, magic mixes with tears and laughter....and life becomes real.

i matter

it was when she first dared to see
her truth, that the winds howled.
after a time, it strengthened her
and she spoke her truth
and the earth shook.
and when finally,
she believed her truth –
the stars rejoiced,
the universe opened,
and even her bones sang her song:
"I Matter!"

for amy

alone and shaking,
she wondered how she'd get thru.
the doubts surrounding her, keeping her awake.
and then she remembered.
it's all a ride, a journey, a dream.
the twists and turns of which she
couldn't even fathom.
she closed her eyes and rested.
she'd travel where she must.
never knowing where she was going...
but knowing it was a ride worth taking.

inner wisdom

your inner voice is the voice of the soul...follow it.

nothing

they sat around me encircling me with
compassion and wisdom.
bandaging the wounds made in the name of love.
over and over they claim
"it's nothing."
well, then....
give me "nothing" over "love" any day.

her angels

this was a new twist of the road.
such a dark and complicated twist.
she could think of only one kind of guide to lead her thru -
she called on her angels
and leaned heavily on their wings.

becoming the crone

she bowed her head,
"i don't think the pain will ever go away."
"it won't," he said as he lifted her chin.
"you will always carry it in your heart,
and one day it will make you the
wise old crone you wish to become.
use it. embrace it. and grow with me."

my women friends

there's nothing like my
women friends.
launching straight into matters
of the heart and soul the moment
we're alone.
we use tears, laughter
and wisdom to cross entire
universes in moments.
always arriving back to
where we started -
but never arriving home
completely the same.

heaviness

it feels so heavy
when that door closes –
hard to believe we'll be dancing
thru new ones.
but dance we will.
because somehow this heaviness will
add strength to our dance steps –
if only we let it.

perhaps

perhaps power is letting go of the grip of the past
and standing empty handed facing the future.

opening

it was her heart she needed to open –
not the door.
the door was wide open –
all she needed to do was dare.

my kids

they know me in a way no one else ever has.
they open me to things i never knew existed.
they drive me to insanity
and push me to my depths.
they are the beat of my heart,
the pulse in my veins,
and the energy in my soul.
they are my kids.

her power

she took her power back ~
without permission.

her trees

they plowed down her trees and she wept.
they forgot to take the sky tho.
the clouds became her refuge.

my star sister

quietly she speaks her wisdom ~
then sits back and waits.
trusting and patient,
she loves me into growth.

the festival

they came and went
purchasing their trinkets
captured by the glint of silver,
never seeing the shimmer
under her veil.
i sat and watched her
and prayed she would at least see it.

journeys

she had made it to that mountain peak
that had seemed so far away!
she leaped, danced and rejoiced!
and then quietly, holding a pebble
from that sacred spot, she took her first
step towards the rest of the mountain range.

blame

"who will take the blame?" she asked.
"nobody." he answered.
"it is too much to carry.
leave it behind and let the wind take it.
we have places to go."

her place

she stumbles,
they catch her -
holding her up.
another struggles,
she's surrounded by the love
she's given out.
it's a circle of women
giving, taking and growing
and it is within that circle
she finds her place.

compassion

she finally came to realize
she gave compassion to everyone but herself.
maybe, she thought,
sometimes you don't see something
until you have the strength to act on what
you see.
and she knew now the compassion would come.

her son

she listened to their struggle with pain at first.
and then amazement
as she watched her son become a man.

prayer

for clarity of sight -
to see herself and her intentions -
for this she prayed.

the thaw

there was a time the ice had saved her -
now only the thaw could.

responsibility

after all,
she did allow it, didn't she?
if she allowed it,
did she believe they were right?
time to face her beliefs honestly.
and her responsibility to herself.

all along

it was in her strength to go find the
love for herself, she saw she really
had it all along.

if

if she really believed it –
if she really trusted it –
well, then, it was time
she really lived it.

tables

she looked at him and didn't know who he was.
she never did know, did she?
ah, but now she knew who she was.
at least there weren't two strangers at the table anymore –
only one.
she moved to another table.

shade

resting in the shade of her trust,
she dreamed her dreams –
and then got up to live them.

brambles

it wasn't that she had started
out in the brambles –
that's just where she found
herself now.
with the light shining thru the entanglement.
naming thorn after thorn,
and releasing them,
she found her way to the clearing.

the open fist....

and the fist became the open hand.
she refused to beat herself any longer.
speaking words of kindness,
she gently touched her hair,
looked into her own eyes and
took the first step towards love.

on her own

she felt separated again.
on her own again.
it wasn't that it was bad -
it just took adjusting.

the all

melting,
i lose the me,
and begin to touch the all.

solo flight

it is in your solo flight that your
wings become filled with power,
the clouds part, and the heavens open.

beyond

going beyond acceptance
into a knowing,
she laughed with delight!

grace

maybe grace is figuring out it's not
all about you.
that people are doing what they're
doing for their own reasons.
not yours.
and maybe grace is accepting that.

clouds

soft and white and pure
the clouds surrounded her.
an entire world of magic outside her window –
if only she looked.

high dive

it was a dive off of a very high cliff –
into the depths below.
knowing it was her only chance at living,
she closed her eyes and dove
and trembled every bit of the way.

shaky landing

even after she landed, she trembled.
wanting guarantees
and knowing there were none,
she vowed to keep diving
until guarantees no longer mattered.

choices

believing that every thought counts,
every word matters,
and every action is power –
she chose to fill them
with gentleness and love.

so many years ago

it was so many years ago,
she thought she was over it.
until the day she realized
she had never held it.

mother and child

i look at you and see
reflections of me.
i look again and
i've disappeared.
you are part of me
and i'm a part of you.
we are co-mingled
and yet stand alone.
there is no other miracle
quite like a mother and child.

another passage

she had changed.
they hadn't.
so why was she still hanging around?
she closed her eyes,
wished them well,
wiped her tears
and headed thru another passage
towards her light.

her reason

she had a reason for living now.
her reason.
no one else's.
just hers.
and this she knew,
would take her to the stars –
if only she allowed it.

the safe place

the key was in her hand.
the door within her grasp.
the room stood still,
waiting for her to enter.
trusting it,
trusting the "us" that they'd created,
trusting herself...
she entered.

the game

it was the nature of the game –
while the love was there surrounding him,
the work was his alone.
the journey would be solitary
and the flight extraordinary.

two feet in

it was time for two feet in,
a jump with both feet
and a knowing it's where she belonged.

heaven and earth

sometimes it was so dark,
she just had to believe it was there –
sometimes it was so blinding
all she could do was rejoice.
she traveled between heaven and earth often.

letting them go

she had carried them
with her the whole time
trying to put them down
but never fully letting go.
until now.
it shook her to her very core -
and she knew it was time.

admitting it

she thought she had a decision to make,
but it had already been made.
she felt it inside her.
now she just had to admit it.

the color dance

lacing the orange thru her hair, she laughed.
the purple would make a delightfully long,
soft scarf with light lavender strings poking
out all over the place.
she needed the white across her heart.
and a skirt that twirled in deep dark red.
stripped green and blue socks, the colors of the ocean
and sky would wind around her legs...
and yellow would cover her feet as she danced the dance
of Life once again.

my little girl

i went back and got her today.
the little girl that is me.
i coaxed her to stand,
to drop the blanket,
and to pick up her beauty.
she's walking with me now,
and leading me to wholeness.

her pocket

finding hope in the oddest places,
she tucked it in her pocket.
holding it tight when she was scared,
gently touching it when she was not –
she offered it to her world.

rain, tears and tea

walking thru the rain,
her tears joined the raindrops.
pretty soon there was nothing left to do
but dry off and have a cup of tea.

offering

maybe offering something to the world is living
what you would want to offer.
maybe it's not any more than living it.
and maybe that's the hardest thing of all.......

empty buckets

her bucket emptied.
she had no more to give.
it wasn't a bad thing -
because now she could
walk away.

glimpses

a glimpse of the divine –
and the quest was on.

all this time

all this time she thought she
had been exploring the corridors
of her self.
she finally got to the place where
she realized she had only just
found the door to enter!

mothering

no one ever told her
about this thing called "mothering."
maybe because it was a journey
of discovery –
her greatest work of art…
her biggest lesson in letting go…
where she'd learn to nurture a "self"
to shine bright
and find her own self in the process.
no one can tell you that.
you have to live it to know it.
and when you do,
it changes you forever.

peace

stepping out of the fear,
into the love,
she found peace.

letting them go

watching them,
she saw their hearts and loved them.
knowing herself,
she stepped back and let them go.

staring at the mirror

she had never wanted to see them as part of her -
never wanting to own their weaknesses.
shutting them out in entirety.
until today.
looking in the mirror she saw their features -
and beyond.
she saw their humanness.
staring at the mirror, she claimed them.
staring at the mirror, she honored their part in her.

running with the wind

the shame was gone.
she was stunned.
where did it go?
what should she do?
she ran outside with the wind
and wept with joy.

that afternoon

she had noticed something early that day,
her willingness to look was whole hearted.
her patience and gentleness with herself
freely there.
she knew she would go where she needed.
maybe that was the work.
maybe that's where the growth had come.
and maybe that's what finally gave her
peace that afternoon.

just be

she suddenly saw it -
right in front of her -
she didn't have to convince anyone of
anything.
all she had to do was be.
just be.
the rest would take care of itself.

let it

sometimes the light can just
shine bright.
and sometimes it needs to burn
its way thru the ashes.
either way,
it will come out –
if you let it.

her selves

knowing now they would be seen,
her selves stood before her.
circling her in love –
they claimed their right to be.

acceptance

it finally occurred to her -
accepting others didn't mean
shutting down her true feelings
towards them -
it meant accepting her reaction to them
as much as accepting them!
it meant accepting her feelings as well!
this changed everything -
she inhaled the long forgotten feeling
of freedom and began again.

more than anything

more than anything –
i want to trust a journey
that i don't understand.

the universe

and the universe listened....

starting up again

the universe listened.
she listened.
and the dance that had been quiet
for so long inside of her
began again.

hooks

at first she yanked them out slowly,
laying them in patterns.
feeling their importance.
now, they weren't what mattered anymore.
it was getting thru that cloud that counted.
brushing the hooks off her arms,
scraping them off her body she gave them
little thought.
throwing them aside,
she gathered herself and headed for the
other side of the mist.

making space

it is the act of allowing good things to come
that lives are transformed.

umbrella rides

never quite sure where the wind
will take her,
but gathering insights
from every ride
she's learning to hold on
to her umbrella
and fly.

dancing

it took years for her to dance
but she finally began...
spirit leading, body following.
body flowing, spirit soaring.
losing her self, becoming her all ~
she truly danced for the first time
in her life ~
and she knew joy!

the colors came back

one after another they came and lay their
heavy gray blankets upon her...
finally, the weight and the gray became too much.
thru her tears, she gave up and asked for help.
it was then that the colors came back.

softness

laying her head on her pillow,
she smiled.
she really was learning to
take care of herself.
it was about time, she thought.
her pillow felt extra soft
as she fell asleep.

thanksgiving

she closed her eyes
and thought of her year.
it couldn't be just the "good" she was
thankful for.
it had to be the "all"...
the fullness, the depths, the journey.
the dance of Life.
for these she gave thanks.

souls

she didn't just survive -
she became.

being love

maybe being love is knowing you're okay -
that they can't hurt you...
knowing the power to hurt you is yours alone.
then maybe being love is using your power
to offer compassion.
all they while knowing they're okay too.

strength

strength lies in the
opening of the heart…

trust and opening

trust walked up to opening
and gently tapped her on the shoulder.
may i have this dance? he asked.
smiling shyly, she wrapped her arms
around him.
whirling to the rhythms,
melding with the music,
they danced their way into truly living.

welcome home

standing up after the earthquake,
she saw everything had changed.
one world had crumbled to ashes
while another had grown solid and real.
clouds of peace surrounded it.
love supported it
and forgiveness dwelt among it.
looking up at the gate as she entered
she read the words, "welcome home."

terri didn't know she was a writer, didn't know she was an artist, she just plain ol' didn't know a heck of a lot of anything. and then some good ol' fashioned, gut wrenching, heart ripping pain gripped her life, and she started to discover things about herself.

she began her journey inward. when the pain got to be too much for her, she spilled out her feelings on paper. wanting to honor those feelings somehow, she added art to them. it was with that mixing of spilling and honoring that bone sighs were born.

needing to find a way to support herself and her sons, she began peddling her watercolor bone sighs shop to shop. thru an amazing journey of tears, miracles, trust, terror, laughter, squeezing her eyes closed tight, and following her heart, somehow bone sigh arts became a real business.

home made books were offered for awhile among her prints and cards. cumbersome to make and lacking the desired quality, there came a time when the books needed to become "real." grabbing her sons, terri and the guys decided to go into print!

without terri's sons, bone sigh arts/books would never ever have become what it has. funny how the very reason for the business became what made the business successful. those boys are everything to both terri and bone sighs!

josh is the oldest. an old soul musician, born entertainer, and a loveable guy! yo yo is their gentle giant who's turning into the world's best graphic designer! and zakk is the logical one. computer geek and mad inventor with the marshmallow heart.

and! the boys have expanded into beginning their own businesses for themselves! (check out the information page for a listing of their websites!)

it's been quite a journey for them all.

terri's still scratchin' her head wonderin' if she'll ever figure any of it out! probably not....but she'll keep trying anyway!

- *info* -

terri st.cloud
15809 menk rd
accokeek md 20607
granolastew@gmail.com

bone sigh arts
BoneSighArts.com

bone sigh books
BoneSighBooks.com

Zakk and Yo's business
Mazuzu.com

Yohan's business
BFG-Productions.com

Josh's business
Poodleman.com

CPSIA information can be obtained
at www.ICGtesting.com
Printed in the USA
FSHW020621120819
60915FS

9 780981 544052